M000084169

[Jesus said,] "But when you pray, go to your inner room, close the door, and pray to your Father in secret. And your Father who sees in secret will repay you."

MATTHEW 6:6

Too many of us need to see punishment befall the wicked. For those who feel that way, knowing that good shall have its day isn't reward enough. No. The bad must also be punished.

All that worry that somebody might be getting away with something and all that anxiety that God might not be an exacting judge suggest that revenge-seekers, like the older brother in the Prodigal Son parable, might be doing a lot of things right but are missing something important inside themselves. They may be dutiful and moral but bitter underneath and unable to enter the circle of celebration and the dance.

If we feel wounded and bitter, we're apt to worry that God's justice might be too lenient, with inadequate punishment accorded to the bad. The start of Lent on Ash Wednesday is a good time to give up that way of thinking forever. Doing so means less worry about God's way and more about our own incapacity to forgive, to let go of our hurts, to take delight in life, to give others the gaze of admiration, to celebrate, and to join in the dance. For us to be fit for heaven, bitterness must go.

We may have never really felt in our hearts the true and gentle words that the Father spoke to the older brother of the Prodigal Son: "My son, you are here with me always; everything I have is yours. But now we must celebrate and rejoice, because your brother was dead and has come to life again" (Luke 15:31–32).

I have set before you life and death, the blessing and the curse. Choose life, then, that you and your descendants may live.

DEUTERONOMY 30:19

A quality that endeared Henri Nouwen to the world was his candor about his own shortcomings and his refusal to pretend he was anything other than what he was: a sincere, weak man struggling to live his life in honesty.

There were seasons in his life when Nouwen wouldn't go on the road alone to give talks and conferences. He had a sense of community and wanted a core member from his community to share the experience with him. But the humble Nouwen was also honest enough to know that he couldn't always fully trust himself to travel alone. The presence of family and community can be a powerful moral watchdog on our behavior. Nouwen understood this.

Too often we lack that kind of humility and honesty and consequently have things to hide. The little or big secrets we tuck away keep us from full moral health.

The human spirit is not made to live in dishonesty and duplicity. When we do wrong, we either have to stop doing wrong or at least own up to our weakness and be contrite. If we don't get honest, our spirits will begin to harden and warp. Such is the anatomy of the soul. This Lent and always, let's let go of any duplicity, and get and stay honest.

Is this not, rather, the fast that I choose: / releasing those bound unjustly, untying the thongs of the yoke; / Setting free the oppressed, / breaking off every yoke?

ISAIAH 58:6

Too few of us admit that we carry a lot of anger inside of us, that there are places in us that are bitter and resentful, and that there are certain incidents in our lives that we won't forget and people we won't forgive.

To camouflage our anger, we like to make a public display of our generosity and goodness. We tend to make a show to family and friends of how nice we are by praising someone lavishly and then, almost in the same sentence, call someone else a name, slander someone, or speak viciously or sarcastically about someone.

This proclivity to divide others into either angels or demons is a sure indication that anger is inside of us. We make a display of praising certain people that's really meant more to publicly exhibit how nice we are than to highlight someone else's virtues. Then we complain bitterly about how awful some other people are and how we are forever surrounded with idiots. Both the praise and the complaint testify to the same thing. We are living with anger.

Honesty and humility should eventually bring us to admit this. We all carry some anger, and we should not deceive ourselves on this. We need courage and honesty to face up to the anger and do our best—with the help of God—to let it go.

The Lord will guide you always / and satisfy your thirst in parched places, / will give strength to your bones / And you shall be like a watered garden, / like a flowing spring whose waters never fail.

ISAIAH 58:11

As human beings, we're weak and lack the moral strength to always act according to what's best in us. Sometimes we just succumb to temptation, to weakness. Sin needs no explanation beyond this: we're human!

Also, sometimes people are caught in sinful situations they didn't create. They've been abused, made to live in sinful circumstances not of their own choosing, are victims of trafficking, are victims of unjust familial or social situations, or are deeply wounded in other ways that keep them from actualizing their own moral faculties. In situations like this, wrong action is a question of survival, not of free choice. In these cases, generally, beneath an understandably hardened, calloused surface lies a still-innocent heart that clearly knows its need for God's mercy. There *is* such a thing as honest sin.

There's also sin that's dishonest, rationalized, that's forever buffered by a phony pride that can't admit its own sinfulness. The result then, most often, is a hardened, bitter, judgmental soul. When sin is rationalized, bitterness will invariably follow, accompanied by hatred toward the kind of virtue from which it has fallen. When we rationalize, our moral DNA will not let itself be fooled. It reacts and punishes us by having us hate ourselves. And when someone hates himself, that hatred will issue forth in a hatred of others and, more particularly, in a hatred of the exact virtue from which he has fallen.

Giving up false pride for Lent and for all time helps us find ourselves as weak and sinful, which can soften our hearts, make us humble, and open us to receive God's mercy.

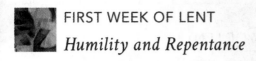

FIRST WEEK OF LENT
Humility and Repentance

First Sunday of Lent

Beloved, do not look for revenge but leave room for the wrath; for it is written,
"Vengeance is mine, I will repay, says the Lord."

ROMANS 12:19

As a child on the farm, I recall seeing folks break a horse
brought in from the wild. Colts that had run free would be caught and
forced to submit to a halter, a saddle, and commands. The process of
breaking the horse's freedom and spirit was far from gentle, and yielded a
mixed result. The horse was now compliant, but part of its spirit was gone.

That's an apt image for the journey, both human and spiritual.
Life, in ways that are far from gentle, eventually breaks our spirit, for
good and for bad, and we end up humble, but we also end up somewhat
wounded and unable to—metaphorically—stand upright.

Because of the pain of our brokenness, we focus more on ourselves
than on others, and we end up disabled. Bruised and fragile, we're
unable to properly give and receive. We stutter, reticent to share the
goodness and depth of our own persons.

Perhaps when the priest blesses the congregation at the end of a
liturgy, instead of saying, "Bow down for the blessing," he might say
instead, "Those of you who think you are not in need of this blessing,
please bow your heads and pray for God's blessing. Meanwhile, those of
you who feel beaten, broken, and unworthy of this blessing, raise your
heads to receive a love and a gift that you have long despaired of ever
again receiving."

FIRST MONDAY OF LENT

Take no revenge and cherish no grudge against your own people. You shall love your neighbor as yourself. I am the LORD.

LEVITICUS 19:18

We know it's easy enough to be understanding, loving, and forgiving when you are bathed in them. It's quite another thing when your very adherence to those qualities is making you the object of misunderstanding, hatred, and murder.

In Gethsemane, we see Jesus prostrate, humanly devastated, on the ground, struggling mightily to cling to a cord of sustenance that had always sustained him in trust, love, and forgiveness and had kept paranoia, hatred, and despair at bay. The answer doesn't come easy for him. He has to pray repeatedly and, in Luke's words, "sweat blood" before he can regain his balance and root himself again in that grace that sustained him throughout his ministry. Love and forgiveness are not easy. Not giving in to anger, bitterness, self-pity, hatred, and the desire for vengeance didn't come easy for Jesus, either.

Our ultimate moral struggle is not giving in to our natural reactions whenever we are disrespected, slighted, ignored, misunderstood, hated, or victimized in small or large ways. In the face of these, paranoia automatically takes over and most everything inside us conspires to create an obsessive pressure toward giving back in kind, slight for slight, disrespect for disrespect, ugliness for ugliness, hatred for hatred, violence for violence.

Like Jesus, who himself had to struggle mightily to not give in to coldness and hatred, we also can draw strength through the same umbilical cord that nurtured him. His Father's grace and strength can nurture us, too.

FIRST TUESDAY OF LENT

This is how you are to pray: Our Father in heaven, / hallowed be your name, / your kingdom come, / your will be done, / on earth as in heaven.

MATTHEW 6:9–10

In the early years of the Church, it was thought that the ideal way to die as a Christian was through martyrdom. A rich spirituality developed from martyrdom, which people began to see more metaphorically, such as giving one's blood through selflessness, through sacrificing one's hopes and dreams for others, through giving away one's life through duty, and through letting oneself be constantly called out of one's personal agenda to respond to the needs of others.

If we understood this, we would be happier. When we try to live as if our lives are about ourselves, we either end up too full of ourselves or too empty of everything else, inflated, or depressed. Put simply, we either end up dying in selflessness on one hill or we end up full of ourselves and self-hatred on some other hill!

This longing for martyrdom has various disguises, some lofty and others less so. The desire for martyrdom manifests itself in the desire for heroism, the desire for greatness, the desire to be a great lover, the desire to leave a mark, to be immortal. Underpinning all of these is the desire to take love and meaning to their ultimate, altruistic end, death in sacrifice for others.

This is the deep, instinctual pattern written into the soul itself, and it posits that real maturity lies in being stretched truly tall, on some cross, in crucifixion.

FIRST WEDNESDAY OF LENT

A clean heart create for me, God; / renew within me a steadfast spirit.

PSALM 51:12

In Luke's Gospel, we read that Jesus, on the night before he died, went to the Garden of Gethsemane with his disciples. There he invited them to pray with him as he struggled to find the strength to face his death. But as Luke cryptically adds, while Jesus sweat blood, he was "a stone's throw from them" (Luke 22:41).

How far is a stone's throw? Its distance is enough to leave you in a place where no one can reach you. Jesus faced his death knowing he was loved by others but also knowing that in the face of death he was entering a place where he was deeply and utterly alone. It is within that utter aloneness that Jesus has to continue to give himself over in trust, love, forgiveness, and faith.

It was not the capacity to physically endure scourging and nails that was the real test inside of Jesus' passion. Jesus' agony in the Garden was rather about how he would die: Could he continue to surrender himself to a God and to a truth he had previously known when this now seemed to be belied by everything around him? Could he continue to trust? What kind of spirit would he hand over at the end? Would it be gracious or bitter? Forgiving or vengeful? Loving or hate-filled? Trusting or paranoid? Hope-filled or despairing?

That also will be our test in the end. One day each of us will have to give over his or her spirit. Will our hearts be warm or bitter?

FIRST THURSDAY OF LENT

*Do to others whatever you would have them do to you. This is the law and
the prophets.*

MATTHEW 7:12

It's interesting to note that in the famous text on the Final
Judgment in the Gospel where Jesus describes how God will divide the
sheep from the goats on the basis of how they treated the poor, neither
group—those who did it correctly and those who didn't—actually knew
what they were doing.

The group who did it right stated they didn't know that in touching
the poor they were touching Christ. The group that got it wrong
protested that had they known that Christ was in the poor, they would
have reached out. Jesus assures us it doesn't matter. Mature discipleship
lies simply in the doing, regardless of our conscious attitude.

We need to be alert not just to our conscious attitudes but to what
we are actually doing. We can—in all sincerity, in all good conscience,
in all good heart—be blind toward justice and the poor. We can be
moral men and women, pious churchgoers, generous donors to those
who ask help from us, and warm to our own families and friends. Yet at
the same time we can be blind to ourselves, though not to the poor; be
unhealthily elitist, subtle racists, callous toward the environment, and
protective of our own privilege. We are still good persons no doubt,
but the absence of compassion in one area of our lives leaves us limping
morally.

How will our goodness be judged? How do we treat the poor, and
how well do we love our enemies?

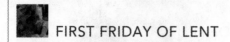
FIRST FRIDAY OF LENT

For with the LORD is mercy, / with him is plenteous redemption.

PSALM 130:7

When we look at church life today, especially within parishes, it is obvious that it is made up of much more than only the core, committed congregation, namely those who participate regularly in church life and accept (at least for the main part) the dogmatic and moral teachings of their churches.

The church also contains a wide variety of the less-engaged: people who practice occasionally, people who accept some of its teachings, guests who visit our churches, people who don't explicitly commit but are sympathetic to the Church and offer it various kinds of support, and; not least, people who link themselves to God in more private ways, those who are spiritual but not religious.

This does not mean that there are tiers within discipleship, where some are called to a higher holiness and others to a lower one. The Church may never be divided into the perfect and less perfect, the better and the half-baked, full participation and partial participation. The full gospel applies to everyone, as does Jesus' invitation to intimacy with him. Christian discipleship doesn't ideally admit of levels, notches, layers, and different tiers of participation. Each individual chooses how deep he or she will go. Some go deeper than others, though everyone is meant to go its full depth.

We are all around Jesus in our different ways, and we must be careful not to judge each other.

FIRST SATURDAY OF LENT

Today you have accepted the Lord's agreement: he will be your God, and you will walk in his ways, observe his statutes, commandments, and ordinances, and obey his voice.

DEUTERONOMY 26:17

Among Jesus' many teachings we find this rather harsh-sounding invitation: "Whoever wishes to come after me must deny himself, take up his cross, and follow me" (Matthew 16:24).

Part of that means accepting that suffering is a part of our lives. Accepting our cross and giving up our lives means that, at some point, we have to make peace with the unalterable fact that frustration, disappointment, pain, misfortune, illness, unfairness, sadness, and death are part of our lives and must ultimately be accepted without bitterness. As long as we nurse the notion that pain in our lives is something we need not accept, we will habitually find ourselves bitter because we did not accept the cross.

Taking up your cross and being willing to give up your life means living in a faith that believes nothing is impossible for God. Indeed, whenever we succumb to the notion that God cannot offer us a way out of our pain into some kind of newness, it's precisely because we have reduced God down to the size of our own limited imagination. It's only possible to accept our cross, to live in trust, and to not grow bitter inside pain if we believe in possibilities beyond what we can imagine, namely if we believe in the resurrection.

We can take up our cross when we begin to believe in the resurrection.

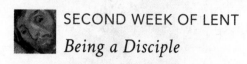

SECOND WEEK OF LENT
Being a Disciple

Second Sunday of Lent

So do not be ashamed of your testimony to our Lord, nor of me, a prisoner for his sake; but bear your share of hardship for the gospel with the strength that comes from God.

2 TIMOTHY 1:8

Today, among many of us churchgoers, there is a growing propensity to self-protect rather than risk crucifixion for the world. We are well-intentioned in this, but, good intentions notwithstanding, our actions are the opposite of Jesus. He loved the world enough to let himself be crucified rather than self-protect.

Jesus' disciples were forever trying to protect him from various groups they deemed unworthy of his presence, and Jesus was forever clear that he didn't need or want to be protected.

More importantly, his disciples were also trying to protect him against persons and things they deemed as threats to him. What was Jesus' response to this effort at protection? We have his words: no more of this! But we don't have the tone of those words. Were they spoken in anger, as sharp reprimand? Were they spoken in frustration, recognizing that Peter, the rock, the future pope, had so badly misunderstood his message? Or were they spoken in that sad tone a mother uses when she tells her children to stop fighting even as the resignation in her voice betrays the fact that she knows they never will? Whatever the tone, the message is clear that his first followers didn't understand one of the central things about their master: Jesus had spent his entire ministry healing people, including healing diseased ears so that people might hear again. And, on his last night on earth the leader of his apostles cuts off the ear of someone in an attempt to protect him.

Everything about Jesus speaks of vulnerability rather than self-protection. He was born in a manger, a feeding trough, a place where animals come to eat, and he ends up on a table, "flesh for the life of the world," to be eaten up by the world (John 6:51). The first words out of his mouth call for metanoia, the opposite of paranoia. In the end, he gives himself over to crucifixion rather than to self-protection. That was Jesus' response to a world that grossly misunderstood him and violently mistreated him. He opened his arms in vulnerability rather than closed his fists in self-defense.

Ideally, that's how we should respond when the world is unfair to us. Unlike Peter, who failed to remember Jesus' message and instinctively struck with his sword, don't let threats erase what was central to Jesus' teaching by responding in a manner antithetical to the gospel, hostility for hostility, immaturity for immaturity.

Jesus loved the world enough to let himself be crucified rather than self-protect.

SECOND MONDAY OF LENT

Be merciful, just as [also] your Father is merciful.

LUKE 6:36

In the letters of St. Paul, the apostle makes a distinction between life in the flesh as opposed to life in the Spirit.

Life in the flesh is characterized by lewd conduct, impurity, licentiousness, idolatry, sorcery, hostilities, bickering, jealousy, outbursts of rage, selfish rivalries, dissensions, factionalism, envy, drunkenness, and orgies (see Galatians 5:16–21). When these exist in our lives, Paul cautions, we may not delude ourselves into thinking we are living inside of God's spirit.

"In contrast, the fruit of the Spirit is love, joy, peace, patience, kindness, generosity, faithfulness, gentleness, self-control. Against such there is no law" (Galatians 5:22–23). It is only when these qualities are manifest in our lives that we may understand ourselves as walking in true discipleship.

For Paul, the litmus test for discipleship is not a single moral issue but rather a whole way of living that radiates more love than selfishness, more joy than bitterness, more peace than factionalism, more patience and respect than negative judgment and gossip, more empathy than anger, and more willingness to sweat the blood of sacrifice than to give in to the temptations of the moment.

Christian discipleship is not just about our actions; it's also about our hearts. The essence of Christian discipleship lies in putting on the heart of Christ. Proper morality, defense of truth, and life-giving Church practices follow from that—and, when rooted in that, they become respectful, forgiving, and loving.

SECOND TUESDAY OF LENT

*Learn to do good. / Make justice your aim: redress the wronged, / hear the
orphan's plea, defend the widow.*

ISAIAH 1:17

Those of us who are parents, ministers, teachers, catechists,
and elders must risk proclaiming the prodigal character of God's mercy.
We must not spend God's mercy as if it were ours, dole out God's
forgiveness as if it were a limited commodity, put conditions on God's
love as if God were a petty tyrant or a political ideology, or cut off access
to God as if we were the keeper of the heavenly gates. We aren't.

It is interesting to note in the Gospels how the well-meaning
apostles often tried to keep certain people away from Jesus as if they
weren't worthy, as if they were an affront to his holiness or would
somehow stain his purity. They perennially tried to prevent children,
prostitutes, tax collectors, known sinners, and the uninitiated of all
kinds from coming to Jesus. But Jesus always overruled their attempts
with words like: Let them come! I want them to come.

We need to do more in risking God's mercy. The place of justice
and truth should never be ignored, but we must risk letting the infinite,
unbounded, unconditional, undeserved mercy of God flow free.

Like the apostles, we are well-intentioned, forever trying to keep
certain individuals and groups away from God's mercy as it is offered
in word, sacrament, and community. God doesn't want our protection.
What God does want is for everyone, regardless of morality, orthodoxy,
lack of preparation, age, or culture, to come to the unlimited waters of
divine mercy.

SECOND WEDNESDAY OF LENT

The Son of Man did not come to be served but to serve and to give his life as a ransom for many.

MATTHEW 20:28

With the current state of affairs, whether you're looking at politics or the churches, it's a challenge not to become pessimistic, angry, and bitter. But bitterness and anger, no matter how justified, are not good places to stay. Both Jesus and what's noble inside of us invite us to move beyond anger and indignation.

At the truly bitter moments of our lives—when we're feeling overwhelmed by feelings of misunderstanding, slight, injustice, and rightful indignation and we're staring across at those whom we deem responsible for the situation—anger and hatred will naturally arise within us. It's OK to dwell with them for a time because anger is an important mode of grieving. But after a time we need to move on. The challenge is to ask ourselves: How do I love now, given all this hatred? What does love call me to now in this bitter situation? Where can I now find a common thread that can keep me in family with those at whom I'm angry? How do I reach through the space that now leaves me separated by my own justified feelings of anger? And perhaps most important of all: Where can I now find the strength to not give in to hatred and self-serving indignation?

That's the ultimate moral challenge, the test that Jesus himself faced in Gethsemane. How do you love when everything around you invites you to the opposite?

SECOND THURSDAY OF LENT

Blessed are those who trust in the LORD; / the LORD will be their trust.

JEREMIAH 17:7

Life is tough, and it can be grossly unfair sometimes. Perhaps
the greatest unfairness of all is not the injustice of being victimized,
violated, raped, or murdered, but that—after all this has been done
to us—we're expected to forgive the one who did it to us while at the
same time knowing that he may well have an easier time of it in terms
of letting go of the incident and moving toward reconciliation. That's
perhaps the greatest unfairness of all.

And yet this is the invitation to all of us who have ever been
victimized. American author Parker Palmer suggests that violence is
what happens when someone doesn't know what else to do with his or
her suffering and that domestic abuse, racism, sexism, homophobia, and
contempt for the poor are all cruel outcomes of this. What we need, he
suggests, is bigger "moral imagination."

Understanding that our abuser may be in deep agony, that the bully
himself was first bullied, doesn't generally do much to ease our own
pain and humiliation. Plus, imagining how ideally we should respond
as Christians is helpful, but by itself it doesn't give us the strength to
forgive. Something else is needed, namely a strength that's now beyond
us.

This is a tough teaching, one that should not be presented glibly.
How do you forgive someone who violated you? In this life, mostly, it's
impossible; but there may be a time when, finally, with God's help, we
will be able to bridge that unbridgeable chasm.

SECOND FRIDAY OF LENT

*Therefore, I say to you, the kingdom of God will be taken away from you
and given to a people that will produce its fruit.*

MATTHEW 21:43

Saint Augustine teaches that we can never be morally neutral.
We are either growing in virtue or falling into vice. We never have
the luxury of simply being in a holding state. Either we are growing in
goodness or sliding in the opposite way. That's true for all of life.

So also with our attitude toward justice and the poor: either we are
actively reaching out to the poor and being more drawn into concern
for them or we are unconsciously hardening our hearts against them
and unknowingly sliding into attitudes that trivialize their issues
and distance ourselves from them. If we are not actively advocating
for justice and the poor, it is inevitable that at a point we will, with
completely sincere hearts, downplay the issues of poverty, racism,
inequality, and injustice.

We can, in all good conscience and with a good heart, be blind
toward justice and the poor. As I have stated before, we can be moral
men and women, pious churchgoers, generous donors to those who
seek help from us, and warm to our own families and friends. Yet at
the same time we can be blind to ourselves, though not to the poor; be
unhealthily elitist, subtle racists, callous toward the environment, and
protective of our own privilege. We are still good persons no doubt,
but the absence of compassion in one area of our lives leaves us limping
morally.

SECOND SATURDAY OF LENT

Shepherd your people with your staff, / the flock of your heritage, / That lives apart in a woodland, / in the midst of an orchard. / Let them feed in Bashan and Gilead, / as in the days of old; / As in the days when you came from the land of Egypt, / show us wonderful signs.

MICAH 7:14–15

Orphans, widows, and strangers! That's scriptural code for who, at any given time, are the three most vulnerable groups in society.

Today, without doubt, we are facing the biggest humanitarian crisis since the end of the Second World War. Millions upon millions of people, under unjust persecution and the threat of death, are being driven from their homes and homelands with no place to go and no country or community to receive them.

As Christians, we may not turn our backs on them or turn them away. If Jesus is to be believed, we will be judged spiritually more by how we treat refugees than by whether or not we are going to church. When we stand before God in judgment and ask in protest, "When did I see a stranger and not welcome him?" Our generation may hear God reply, "I was a Syrian refugee, and you did not welcome me."

The issue of refugees and immigrants is highly sensitive and complex. But as we—our churches and our governments—address them, we must remain clear on what the Scriptures, Jesus, and the social teachings of the Church uncompromisingly teach: we are to welcome the stranger, even when it's inconvenient and even if there are dangers.

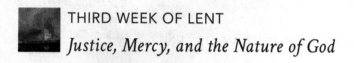

Justice, Mercy, and the Nature of God

Third Sunday of Lent

Indeed, only with difficulty does one die for a just person, though perhaps for a good person one might even find courage to die. But God proves his love for us in that while we were still sinners Christ died for us.

ROMANS 5:7–8

Anyone who has ever watched a fire knows that, at a point, the flames subside and disappear into smoldering coals that themselves eventually cool and turn into cold, gray ash. But there's a moment in that process, before they cool off, that the coals can be stirred in order to make them burst into flame again.

That's the image St. Paul uses to encourage us to rekindle the fires of our faith when they seem to be burning low: "I remind you to stir into flame the gift of God" (2 Timothy 1:6). It's a meaningful image. Our faith sometimes needs some stirring at its roots to make it alive again. How do we do that?

We stir our faith back into flame by resituating ourselves inside its roots. Even though faith is a divine gift, it can be helpful sometimes to journey back and examine what earthly forces helped plant the faith inside us.

Who and what helped give us faith? That's a deeply personal question that each of us can only answer for himself or herself. It could be the faith and witness of our parents, our church community, our teachers, or others who helped us find ways to hear God's voice and left deep, permanent roots in our souls.

But sometimes God's voice can feel completely silent. Sometimes our imagination can run dry so that we don't feel God's presence. It's then that we need to stir the seemingly smoldering coals of our faith by making a journey back to reground ourselves to where our faith found its roots.

This kind of journey can be helpful for most everybody, with one cautionary flag. The seeming silence of God in our lives as adults can in fact be a deeper modality of God's presence rather than a sign of a deteriorating faith. The voice of God often seems clear at times but later on that clarity gives way to what the mystics call the "dark nights of the soul," where God's seeming absence is not a question of a loss of faith but of a new, richer, less-imaginative mode of God's presence in our lives. Fervor is not always a sign of a deep faith, just as the seeming absence of God is not necessarily a sign of a weakening faith. God must be patiently waited for and will arrive in our lives only on God's terms, not ours.

Even so, St. Paul's advice remains: "I remind you to stir into flame the gift of God."

"Stir into flame the gift of God."

THIRD MONDAY OF LENT

As the deer longs for streams of water, / so my soul longs for you, O God.

PSALM 42:2

Anyone who claims to understand God is deceived, because we know that God is ineffable. That means that we can know God, but never adequately capture God in a concept. God is unimaginable. If God could be understood, then God would be as limited as we are.

God may be ineffable, but God's nature *is* known. Divine revelation, as seen through nature, as seen through other religions, and especially as seen through Jesus, spells out what's inside God's inexpressible reality.

What's revealed there is both comforting beyond all comfort and challenging beyond all challenge. What's revealed in the beauty of creation, in the compassion that's the hallmark of all true religion—and in Jesus' revelation of his Father—takes us beyond a blind date into a trustworthy relationship. Nature, religion, and Jesus conspire together to reveal an Ultimate Reality, a Ground of Being, a Creator and Sustainer of the universe, a God who is wise, intelligent, prodigal, compassionate, loving, forgiving, patient, good, trustworthy, and beautiful beyond imagination.

God cannot be deciphered, circumscribed, or captured in human thought; but, from what can be deciphered, we're in good, safe hands. We can sleep well at night. God has our back. In the end, both for humanity as a whole and for our own individual lives. As Julian of Norwich prayed: "All shall be well, and all shall be well, and all manner of thing shall be well." God is good.

THIRD TUESDAY OF LENT

Then Peter approaching asked him, "Lord, if my brother sins against me,
how often must I forgive him? As many as seven times?" Jesus answered,
"I say to you, not seven times but seventy-seven times."

MATTHEW 18:21–22

The Gospels, as we know, reveal a God who is prodigal beyond all our standards and beyond our imagination. The God of the Gospels is the Sower who, because he has unlimited seeds, scatters those seeds everywhere without discrimination: on the road, in the ditches, in the thornbushes, in bad soil, and in good soil.

Moreover, that prodigal Sower is also the God of creation, that is, the God who has created and continues to create hundreds of billions of galaxies and billions of human beings. And this prodigal God gives us this perennial invitation: come to the waters, come without money, come without merit because God's gift is as plentiful, available, and as free as the air we breathe.

The Gospel of Luke recounts an incident where Peter, just after he had spent an entire night fishing and had caught nothing, is told to cast out his net one more time and, this time, Peter's net catches so many fish that the weight of the catch threatens to sink two boats. Peter reacts by falling to his knees and confessing his sinfulness. But as the text makes clear, that's not the proper reaction in the face of overabundance. Peter is wrongly fearful, in effect, wanting that overabundance to go away. Rather, Jesus wants him—in the face of too much—to go into the world and share with others that unimaginable grace.

THIRD WEDNESDAY OF LENT

For what great nation is there that has gods so close to it as the LORD, our God, is to us whenever we call upon him?

DEUTERONOMY 4:7

The Gospels recount an incident where Jesus goes to the synagogue on a Sabbath, stands to read, and quotes a text from Isaiah—except he doesn't quote it fully. He omits a part that would have been known to his listeners. It describes Isaiah's vision of what will be the sign that God has finally broken into the world and irrevocably changed things.

For Isaiah, the sign that God is now ruling the earth will be good news for the poor, consolation for the brokenhearted, freedom for the enslaved, grace abundant for everyone, and vengeance on the wicked. Notice, though, when Jesus quotes this, he leaves out the part about vengeance and seeing the wicked punished.

In heaven we will be given what we're owed and more (unmerited gifts, forgiveness we don't deserve, joy beyond imagining), but it seems we will not be given that catharsis we so much want here on earth: the "joy" of seeing the wicked punished.

We know we need God's mercy, but if grace is true for us, it has to be true for everyone. If forgiveness is given to us, it must be given to everybody. And if God does not avenge our misdeeds, God must not avenge the misdeeds of others, either. Such is the logic of grace and such is the love of God, to whom we must attune ourselves.

THIRD THURSDAY OF LENT

When your days have been completed and you rest with your ancestors,
I will raise up your offspring after you, sprung from your loins, and
I will establish his kingdom.

2 SAMUEL 7:12

Some day you will have to face your Maker! We've all heard that phrase. The hour will come when we will stand alone before God with no place to hide, no room to rationalize, and no excuses to offer for our weaknesses and sin. We will stand in a searing light, naked and exposed, and all we ever did, good and bad, will stand with us in that light. That prospect, however vaguely felt, makes for a dark corner in every person's mind.

But searing judgment of our souls is meant to be a daily occurrence, not a single traumatic moment at the end of our lives. We are meant to bring ourselves, with all our complexities and weaknesses, into God's full light every day. Genuine prayer brings us into that searing light.

We are meant to face God like this every day, not just at the moment of our death. So we should set aside time each day to put ourselves into God's presence without words and without images, where—naked, stripped of everything, silent, exposed, hiding nothing, completely vulnerable—we simply sit, full face, before God's judgment and mercy.

By doing this, we will preempt any traumatic encounter at the time of our death and, more importantly, we will begin—here and now—to enjoy more fully God's empathic embrace.

THIRD FRIDAY OF LENT

Who is wise enough to understand these things? / Who is intelligent enough to know them? / Straight are the paths of the LORD, / the just walk in them, / but sinners stumble in them.

HOSEA 14:10

If the Gospel of John is to be believed—and it is—Jesus judges no one. God judges no one.

That needs to be put into context. It doesn't mean there aren't any moral judgments and that our actions are indifferent to moral scrutiny. There is judgment, except it doesn't work the way it is fantasized inside the popular mind. According to what Jesus is quoted as saying in John's Gospel, judgment works this way: God's light, God's truth, and God's spirit come into the world. We then judge ourselves according to how we live in the face of them: God's light has come into the world, but we can choose to live in darkness. That's our decision, our judgment. God's truth has been revealed, but we can choose to live in falsehood, in lies. That's our decision, our judgment to make.

So then, this is how judgment happens: God's spirit (charity, joy, peace, patience, kindness, goodness, trustfulness, gentleness, and chastity) has been revealed. We can choose to live inside the virtues of that spirit, or we can choose to live instead inside their opposites (self-indulgence, sexual vice, rivalry, antagonism, bad temper, quarrels, drunkenness, and factionalism).

One choice leads to a life with God, the other leads away from God. And that choice is ours to make. It doesn't come from the outside. We judge ourselves. God judges no one. God doesn't need to.

THIRD SATURDAY OF LENT

Come, let us return to the Lord, / For it is he who has torn, but he will heal us; /
he has struck down, but he will bind our wounds.

HOSEA 6:1

There comes a point in life when our spiritual struggle is no
longer with the fact that we are desperately in need of God's forgiveness,
but rather that God's grace and forgiveness is overly lavish, unmerited,
and especially that it goes out so indiscriminately.

God's lavish love and forgiveness go out equally to those who have
worked hard and to those who haven't, to those who have been faithful
for a long time and to those who jumped aboard at the last minute, to
those who have had to bear the heat of the day and to those who didn't,
to those who did their duty and to those who lived selfishly.

God's love isn't a reward for being good, doing our duty, resisting
temptation, bearing the heat of the day in fidelity, saying our prayers,
remaining pure, or offering worship—good and important though these
are.

God loves us because God is love and God cannot *not* love and
cannot be discriminating in love. God's love, as Scripture says, shines on
the good and bad alike. That's nice to know when we need forgiveness
and unmerited love, but it's hard to accept when that forgiveness and
love is given to those whom we deem less worthy of it, to those who
didn't seem to do their duty. It's not easy to accept that God's love does
not discriminate, especially when God's blessings go out lavishly to
those who don't seem to deserve them.

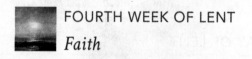

FOURTH WEEK OF LENT
Faith

Fourth Sunday of Lent

For you were once darkness, but now you are light in the Lord. Live as children of light.

EPHESIANS 5:8

Imagine yourself lying in bed some night. You have just had a very good time of prayer and are flooded with feelings and images about God. You have strong, clear feelings that God exists. On that particular evening you have no faith doubts; you can feel the existence of God.

Now, imagine another night, a darker one. You wake up from a fitful sleep and are overwhelmed by the sense that you don't believe in God. You try to convince yourself that you still believe, but you cannot. Every attempt to imagine that God exists and to feel his presence comes up empty. You feel an overwhelming emptiness inside because of that feeling. Try as you might, you cannot shake the feeling that you no longer believe. Try as you might, you can no longer regain the solid ground on which you once stood. Try as you might, you can no longer make yourself feel the existence of God.

Does this mean that on one of these nights you have a strong faith and on the other you have a weak one? Not necessarily. It can just as easily mean that on one night you have a strong imagination and on the other you have a weak one. On one night you can imagine the presence of God and on the other night you cannot. Imagination isn't faith.

We all have had the experience of being inside of certain commitments (marriage, family, church) where, at times, our heads and our hearts are not there, but we are there! The head tells us this doesn't make sense; the heart lacks the proper warm feelings to keep us there. But we remain there, held by something deeper, something beyond what we can explain or feel. This is where faith lives, and this is what faith means.

For long periods, St. Teresa of Calcutta suffered anguish inside of her head and heart every time she tried to imagine the existence of God.

Yet by every indication she lived her whole life in function of God's existence. Her problem was with the limits and poverty of the human imagination. Simply put, she couldn't picture how God exists.

But nobody can because the finite can never picture the infinite, though it can sense it and know it in ways beyond what the head can imagine, and the heart can feel.

Not being able to imagine God's existence is not the same thing as not believing. Our actions are always a more accurate indication of faith than are any of our feelings about God.

Our actions are always a more accurate indication of faith than are any of our feelings about God.

FOURTH MONDAY OF LENT

Instead, shout for joy and be glad forever / in what I am creating. / Indeed, I am creating Jerusalem to be a joy / and its people to be a delight.

ISAIAH 65:18

The deep truth that God loves us unconditionally lies at the heart of our faith. We believe God looks down on our lives and says, "You are my beloved child. In you I take delight!" We do not doubt the truth of that, we just find it impossible to believe.

Unless we are extraordinarily blessed, we rarely, if ever, experience unconditional love. Mostly we experience love with conditions: Our parents love us better when we do not mess up. Our teachers love us better when we behave and perform well. Our churches love us better when we do not sin. Friends love us better when we are successful and not needy. The world loves us better when we are attractive. Our spouses love us better when we do not disappoint them. Mostly, we have to measure up in some way to be loved.

Many of us also have been wounded by supposed expressions of love that weren't love but were expressions of self-serving manipulation, exploitation, or even abuse. We wither under that and become the walking wounded, unable to believe that we are loved and lovable. We know God loves us, so how can we make ourselves believe it?

Deep down, below our wounded parts, the child of God who still inhabits the recesses of our soul knows that he or she is made in God's image and likeness and is special, beautiful, and lovable.

FOURTH TUESDAY OF LENT

Jesus said to him, "Rise, take up your mat, and walk." Immediately the man became well, took up his mat, and walked.

JOHN 5:8–9

We tend to think our faith is strongest at those times when we have emotional feelings attached to our imaginations about God or when it's bolstered and inflamed by feelings of fervor.

Great spiritual writers will tell us that this is a good stage in our faith, but an initial one, commonly experienced when we are neophytes. In the earlier stages of a religious journey, it is common to possess strong images and feelings about God.

They also tell us that, at certain moments of our spiritual journey, God "takes away" our certainty and deprives us of all warm feelings in faith. Saint John of the Cross calls this experience of seemingly losing our faith a "dark night of the soul." This describes the experience where we used to feel God's presence with a certain warmth and solidity, but now we feel like God is nonexistent and we are left in doubt. This is what Jesus experienced on the cross and what St. Teresa of Calcutta wrote of in her journals.

While that darkness can be confusing, it can also be maturing. It can help move us from being arrogant, judgmental, religious neophytes to being humble, empathic men and women, living inside a cloud of unknowing, understanding more by not understanding than by understanding, lost in a darkness we cannot manipulate or control, so as to finally be pushed into genuine faith, hope, and love.

FOURTH WEDNESDAY OF LENT

Form a plan, it shall be thwarted; / make a resolve, it shall not be carried out, / for "With us is God!"

ISAIAH 8:10

In a masterful book on grace, author Piet Fransen suggests that we can test how well we understand grace by gauging our reaction to this story:

> *Imagine a man who, during his whole life, is entirely careless about God and morality. He's selfish, ignores the commandments, ignores all things religious, and is basically consumed with pursuing his own pleasure—wine, sex, and song. Then, just hours before his death, he repents of his irresponsibility, makes a sincere confession, receives the sacraments of the Church, and dies inside that conversion.*

What's our immediate reaction to that story? Isn't it wonderful that he received the grace of conversion before he died? Or, more likely: the lucky beggar, he got away with it! He got to have all that pleasure and still gets to go to heaven!

If we felt the latter emotion, even for a moment, we have never deeply understood the concept of grace. Rather, like the older brother in the Prodigal Son, we are still seeing life away from God's house as fuller than life inside God's house, we're still doing the right things mostly out of bitter duty, and we're secretly envying the amoral. But if this is true, we must be gentle with ourselves. This is an occupational hazard for good, faithful people.

We need to be honest in admitting that, despite our real goodness and fidelity, such a reaction indicates that we're still far from being full saints.

FOURTH THURSDAY OF LENT

The works that the Father gave me to accomplish, these works that I perform testify on my behalf that the Father has sent me.

JOHN 5:36

The poet Rumi suggests that we live with a deep secret that sometimes we know, then not, and then know again. That's a good description of faith. Faith isn't something you nail down and possess once and for all. It goes this way: sometimes you walk on water; sometimes you sink like a stone.

The Gospels testify to this in the story of Peter walking on the water: Jesus asks Peter to step out of a boat and walk across the water to him. At first it works. Peter, unthinking, walks on the water. Then, becoming more conscious of what he's doing, he sinks like a rock. We also see this in the massive fluctuations in belief that Jesus' disciples experience during the forty days after the resurrection. Jesus would appear to them, they would trust he was alive, then he would disappear again, and they would lose their trust and go back to the lives they'd led before they met him. The post-resurrection narratives illustrate the dynamics of faith pretty clearly: You believe it. Then you distrust. Then you believe it again. At least, so it seems on the surface.

To be real, faith need not be explicitly religious, but it can express itself simply in faithfulness, loyalty, and trust. We need to trust the unknown, knowing that we will be OK, no matter that on a given day we might feel like we are walking on water or sinking like a stone. Faith runs deeper than our feelings.

FOURTH FRIDAY OF LENT

Look, he is speaking openly and they say nothing to him. Could the authorities have realized that he is the Messiah?

JOHN 7:26

I believe that God exists, not because I have never had doubts, or because I was raised in the faith by persons whose lives gave deep witness to its truth, or because perennially the vast majority of people on this planet believe in God.

I believe that a personal God exists for more reasons than I can name: the goodness of saints, the hook in my own heart that has never let me go, the interface of faith with my own experience, the courage of religious martyrs throughout history, the stunning depth of Jesus' teachings, the deep insights contained in other religions, the mystical experience of countless people, our sense of connection inside the communion of saints with loved ones who have died, the things we sometimes intuitively know beyond all logical reason, the constant recurrence of resurrection in our lives, the essential triumph of truth and goodness throughout history, the fact that hope never dies, the unyielding imperative we feel inside of ourselves to be reconciled with others before we die, the infinite depth of the human heart, and—yes—even the very ability of atheists and agnostics to intuit that somehow it all still makes sense. All of that points to the existence of a living, personal God.

God isn't found at the end of an empirical test, a mathematical equation, or a philosophical syllogism. God is found, explicitly or implicitly, in living a good, honest, gracious, selfless, moral life, and this can happen inside of religion or outside of it.

FOURTH SATURDAY OF LENT

Yet I was like a trusting lamb led to slaughter, not knowing that they were hatching plots against me.

JEREMIAH 11:19

The stone that rolled away from the tomb of Jesus continues to roll away from every sort of grave. Goodness cannot be held, captured, or put to death. It evades its pursuers, escapes capture, slips away, but forever rises all over the world. Such is the meaning of the resurrection.

We see this already in the earthly life of Jesus. There are a number of passages in the Gospels that give the impression that Jesus was somehow highly elusive and difficult to capture. Early on in his ministry, when his own townsfolk get upset with his message and lead him to the brow of a hill to hurl him to his death, we are told that he slipped through the crowd and went away. Later when the authorities try to arrest him, we are told simply that he slipped away.

These stories of his slipping away are highly symbolic. The lesson is not that Jesus was physically deft and elusive, but rather that the word of God, the grace of God, the goodness of God, and the power of God can never be captured, held captive, or ultimately killed. They are adept. They can never be held captive, can never be killed, and even when seemingly they are killed, the stone that entombs them always eventually rolls back and releases them. Goodness continues to resurrect from every sort of grave.

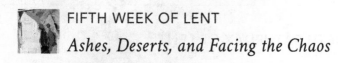

FIFTH WEEK OF LENT

Ashes, Deserts, and Facing the Chaos

Fifth Sunday of Lent

Jesus said to her, "Did I not tell you that if you believe you will see the glory of God?"

JOHN 11:40

Almost all spiritualities have a special place for deserts, wilderness, and other such places where we are unprotected and in danger from untamed nature, wild beasts, and threatening spirits.

In Christian spirituality, these wild places were not meant to lie forever untouched by us and God. The idea was that we men and women of faith were meant to help God finish creation by taming these wilds, exorcizing the bad spirits there, and turning the wilderness into a garden.

In subtle ways, both this concept and its concomitant fears are still with us. What frightens us today is not untamed geography (which we now see as inviting peace and quiet). Rather, for many of us, the untamed, the wilderness, is now visualized more as a gang-infested area within a city, crack houses, singles bars, strip clubs, red-light districts. These are understood as lying outside our cultivated lives, split off from the safety of home and religion, godless places, dangerous, a wilderness.

What frightens us more are the untamed and uncultivated deserts within our own hearts, the unexplored and dark areas inside of us. Like the ancients, we are frightened of what might lie in hiding there, how vulnerable we might be if we entered there, what wild beasts and demons might prey on us there, and whether a chaotic vortex might not swallow us up should we ever venture there. We also fear unexplored places, except our fear is not for our physical safety but for our sanity and our sanctity.

Our Christian faith invites us to go into those areas and turn those dangerous regions into cultivated land, into safe gardens. After all, that is what Jesus did. He went into every dark place, from the singles' bars of his time into death and hell itself, and took God's light and grace there.

But he wasn't naïve. He heeded the advice of the old fairy tales and didn't venture there alone. He entered those underworlds with his hand safely inside his Father's, not walking alone.

Faith is meant to rid us of fear, including fear of the wild beasts and demons that lurk inside the deserts of our minds, hearts, and energies. We are meant to turn those wild, dark areas into safe gardens. But we should heed both our own instincts and the lessons of the old fairy tales: never venture into the dark woods naïvely and alone! Make sure you are armed with a sturdy creed and that you are walking hand-in-hand with your Father.

For many of us, the untamed, the wilderness, is now visualized more as a gang-infested area.

FIFTH MONDAY OF LENT

The Lord, your God, shall you follow, and him shall you fear; his commandments shall you observe.

DEUTERONOMY 13:5

The Gospels tell us that we can reach eternal life only by undergoing the darkness and death of Gethsemane and the cross. The mystics call this the dark night of the soul and assure us that the real transformation of soul does not happen at Disneyland but at Calvary.

However, there can be a dangerous naïvete in all this. The idea is too much that you should just let yourself freefall into the great unknown, with all its darkness and chaos, and growth and happiness are assured. That isn't always true. Far from it.

To enter the darkness, to go into the desert, to face your demons, you must first have the assurance that you will be held by someone or something—God, a loved one, a family, a faith that is strong enough to see your through—while undergoing such a journey.

We see this in Jesus' own paschal journey. He entered the darkness and chaos of Gethsemane and the cross, just as he had once entered the desert, not alone but with another. He was being held by his Father.

Jesus was in the dark night, freefalling, but he wasn't alone. He surrendered himself and jumped over love's cliff, but only because he trusted that someone, his Father, would catch him before he hit the ground. All of us might want to ponder that before we counsel ourselves or others to too hastily abandon safety for chaos. The journey from Disneyland to Calvary should not be undertaken naïvely.

FIFTH TUESDAY OF LENT

[Jesus said,] "The one who sent me is with me. He has not left me alone, because I always do what is pleasing to him."

JOHN 8:29

Much of the Gospels offer a challenge: keep your eyes trained upward, think with your big mind, feel with your big heart, imagine yourself as God's child, mirror that greatness, let Jesus' teachings stretch you, let his spirit fill you, and let high ideals enlarge you.

Spiritualities of the ascent are those that invite us to always strive for what's higher, for what's more noble, for what stretches us and takes us (figuratively) upward beyond the humdrum moral and spiritual ruts within which we continually find ourselves. These spiritualities tell us that sanctity lies in the ascent and that we should habitually stretch ourselves toward higher goals.

But the Gospels also invite us to a spirituality of the descent. They tell us to make friends with the desert, the cross, with ashes, with self-renunciation, with humiliation, with our shadow, and with death itself.

They tell us we grow not just by moving upward but also by descending downward. We also grow by letting the desert work us over, by renouncing cherished dreams to accept the cross, by letting the humiliations that befall us deepen our character, by having the courage to face our own deep chaos, and by making peace with our own mortality.

These spiritualities tell us that sometimes our task, spiritual and psychological, is not to raise our eyes to the heavens, but to look down upon the earth, to sit in the ashes of loneliness and humiliation, to stare down the restless desert inside us.

FIFTH WEDNESDAY OF LENT

[Jesus said,] "If you remain in my word, you will truly be my disciples, and you will know the truth, and the truth will set you free."

JOHN 8:31–32

Before they could enter the Promised Land, Scripture says the Israelites first had to wander in the desert for forty years—letting themselves be led by God, undergoing many trials. The desert came to be seen as the place that correctly shapes the heart, and the idea developed that one should prepare for major transitions by first spending time in the desert.

Later, as the Scriptures developed, the concept of desert was made symbolic. It came to mean more a place in the heart than a place on a map and was understood to be mystical: before you are ready to fully and gratefully receive life, you have to first be readied by facing your own demons, which means going "into the desert," namely entering that place where you are most frightened, lonely, and threatened.

The desert does this for you. It empties you. Hence it is not a place wherein you can decide how you want to grow and change, but is a place that you undergo, expose yourself to, and have the courage to face. The desert purifies you, almost against your will, through God's efforts.

The season of Lent is meant to be a time in the desert to courageously face the chaos and the demons within us. The result is that we are purified, made ready, so that the intoxicating joy of Easter might then serve to bind us more closely to God.

FIFTH THURSDAY OF LENT

God said to Abraham: For your part, you and your descendants after you must keep my covenant throughout the ages.

GENESIS 17:9

After the Last Supper, Jesus goes into the Garden of Gethsemane, where he prays in great agony and, in the face of every kind of resistance within himself, ultimately accepts what his Father asks of him: sacrifice and death.

Scripture says his agony takes place in a garden, archetypically a place of love, where a prince and princess meet to kiss in the moonlight, the place of our dreams, the paradise Adam and Eve lost for us.

Jesus sweats blood there, not as the great teacher or magus, nor as the great king or shepherd, nor even as the great conqueror of sin and death as the divine warrior but as the great lover. In the Garden, Jesus makes the decision to accept something—what will guide his love. This decision costs him blood.

My own dad (who taught me many of the things I trust most deeply about faith and life) used to say, "If you want to keep a commitment, any commitment, you can do it only if you are willing to sweat blood in a garden. To be true to what's asked of you, sometimes you have to make a decision for value that goes against every emotion in your heart." Dad understood what's at stake in the Garden. Tragically, for the most part, we no longer do.

FIFTH FRIDAY OF LENT

But the LORD is with me, like a mighty champion: / my persecutors will stumble, they will not prevail.

JEREMIAH 20:11

In order to deal with the frustrations and tensions that can build up in us, we need to be connected to something beyond ourselves and the situation we're in, such as God, a person, a friendship, a hand, a creed, or a perspective.

Scripture offers wonderful images for this. In the Book of Daniel, three young men are thrown into a blazing furnace. They walked around in the midst of the flames, untouched by the fire because they were singing sacred songs. They sustained their love and faith amid bitter jealousy and hatred by staying connected to something outside of the fiery forces that were consuming everyone else.

Like Jesus and everyone else who's ever walked this planet, we all find ourselves forever inside families, communities, churches, friendships, and work circles that are filled with tension of every kind. Our natural temptation is to simply give back in kind, jealousy for jealousy, gossip for gossip, anger for anger. But what our world really needs is for women and men to step forward and help carry and purify this tension, to help take it away by transforming it inside themselves.

That's not easy for us adults, so when we volunteer to step into the fire, it's wise not to go in alone. Like Jesus, we need to stay connected to some hand, some friend, some creed, and our God who will help sustain us in love and faith, right inside the madness and fire.

FIFTH SATURDAY OF LENT

My dwelling shall be with them; I will be their God, and they will be my people.
EZEKIEL 37:27

Are we ultimately saints or sinners? What's deepest inside us, goodness or selfishness? Or, are we dualists with two innate principles inside us, one good and one evil, in a perpetual duel with each other?

Certainly, at the level of experience, we feel a conflict. There's a saint inside us who wants to mirror the greatness of life, even as there is someone else inside us who wants to walk a seedier path. I like the honesty of Henri Nouwen when he describes this conflict in his own life: "I want to be great saint," he once confessed, "but I don't want to miss out on all the sensations that sinners experience." It's because of this tension inside us that we find it so hard to make clear moral choices. We want the right things, but we also want many of the wrong things. Every choice is a renunciation, and so the struggle between saint and sinner inside us often manifests itself precisely in our inability to make hard choices.

That's part of the mystery of human freedom. The saint and sinner inside us are not separate entities. Rather the saint in us, the big soul, is not only our true self, it's our only self. The sinner in us, the petty soul, is not a separate person or moral force doing perpetual battle with the saint. It's simply the wounded part of the saint, that part of the saint that's been cursed and never properly blessed.

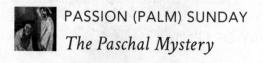

PASSION (PALM) SUNDAY
The Paschal Mystery

The crowds preceding him and those following kept crying out and saying:
"Hosanna to the Son of David; / blessed is he who comes in the name of the
Lord; / hosanna in the highest."

MATTHEW 21:9

In many churches today when the passion is read, the story
is broken up in such a way that one narrator proclaims the overall text,
another person takes the part of Jesus, several others take the parts
of the various people who spoke during his arrest and trial, and the
congregation as a whole is asked to proclaim aloud the parts that were
spoken by the crowds.

For example, in Matthew's account of the trial of Jesus, at a certain
This could not be more appropriate because a congregation in
any Christian church today, and we, as individual members of those
congregations, in our actions and in our words, in countless ways,
mimic perfectly the actions and words of Jesus' contemporaries in their
weaknesses, betrayals, jealousies, religious blindness, and false faith. We
also indict Jesus countless times by how we live.

For example, in Matthew's account of the trial of Jesus, at a certain
moment in the trial, Pontius Pilate comes out to the people, the same
people who just five days before had chanted for Jesus to be their king,
and tells them that, according to custom at Passover time, he is willing
to release one Jewish criminal being held in custody.

Pontius Pilate had in custody a particularly infamous murderer
named Barabbas. So Pilate asks the crowd: "Which one do you want me
to release to you,...Barabbas, or Jesus called Messiah?" (Matthew 27:17).
The crowd roars back, "Barabbas!" Pilate then asks, "Then what shall
I do with Jesus called Messiah?" (Matthew 27:22). The crowd replies
in that verse, "Let him be crucified!" We can make this very obvious
extrapolation: in every moral choice we make, big or small, ultimately
the question we are standing in front of is the same question Pilate
asked the crowd: Whom should I release for you, Jesus or Barabbas?
Graciousness or violence? Selflessness or self-centeredness?

It is the same, of course, with our actions. Like Jesus' disciples, we tend to stay with Jesus more when things are going well, when temptation is not too strong, and when we are not facing real, personal threat. But, like Jesus' original followers, we tend to abandon and betray when things get hard and threatening.

Our spontaneous inclination is to judge very harshly those who surrounded Jesus at his arrest, trial, and sentencing. How could they not see what they were doing? How could they be so blind and jealous? How could they choose false security over God's ultimate shelter? A murderer over the Messiah? How could his followers so easily abandon him?

The choices that those around Jesus made during his trial and sentencing are identical to the choices we make now. And most days we are not doing any better than they did because, still, far too often, given blindness and self-interest, we say, "Let him be crucified!"

Like Jesus' original followers, we tend to abandon and betray when things get hard and threatening.

MONDAY OF HOLY WEEK

Here is my servant whom I uphold, / my chosen one with whom I am pleased. / Upon him I have put my spirit; / he shall bring forth justice to the nations.

ISAIAH 42:1

What does the passion of Jesus mean? As Christians, we believe that Jesus gave us both his life and his death. Too often, however, we do not distinguish between the two, though we should: Jesus gave his life for us in one way, through his activity. He gave his death for us in another way, through his passivity, his passion.

It is easy to misunderstand what the Gospels mean by the passion of Jesus. When we use the word *passion* in relationship to Jesus' suffering, we automatically connect it to the idea of passion as pain—the pain of the crucifixion, of scourging, of whips, of nails in his hands, of humiliation before the crowd.

The passion of Jesus does refer to those, but the word has a different focus here. The English word *passion* takes its root from the Latin *passio*, meaning "passivity," and that's its real connotation here. The word *patient* also derives from passio. Hence, the passion narratives describe Jesus' passivity as "patient." He gives his death to us through his passivity, just as he had previously given his life to us through his activity.

There are many lessons in this, including the fact that life and love are given not just in what we do for others but also, and perhaps even more deeply, in what we absorb at those times when we are helpless, when we have no choice except to be patient.

TUESDAY OF HOLY WEEK

Simon Peter said to him, "Master, where are you going?" Jesus answered [him],
"Where I am going, you cannot follow me now, though you will follow later."

JOHN 13:36

In John's account of the passion, after Jesus dies, soldiers
pierce his side with a lance. Immediately blood and water flow out. This
is a rich image. First of all, it symbolizes birth. When a baby is born,
blood and water accompany the delivery. For John, Jesus' death is the
birth of something new in our lives.

Christians have sometimes been too quick to take this image to
infer the sacraments of baptism and the Eucharist, with the outflow of
blood symbolizing the Eucharist and the outflow of water symbolizing
baptism.

Such an interpretation may be valid, but first there is something
more primal in that image. Blood symbolizes the flow of life inside us.
Water both quenches thirst and washes dirt from our bodies. What
John wants to say with this image is that those who witnessed the death
of Jesus also immediately recognized that the kind of love that Jesus
manifested in dying in this way created a new energy and freedom in
their own lives. They felt both an energy and a cleansing—blood and
water—flowing from Jesus' death. In essence, they felt a power flowing
out of his death into their lives that allowed them to live with less fear,
with less guilt, with more joy, and with more meaning. That is still true
for us today.

John's passion account puts us all on trial and renders a verdict that
frees us from our deepest bondage.

WEDNESDAY OF HOLY WEEK

The Lord GOD is my help, / therefore I am not disgraced; / Therefore I have set my face like flint, / knowing that I shall not be put to shame.

ISAIAH 50:7

Some years ago, my sister, Helen, an Ursuline nun for more than thirty years, died of cancer. Helen loved her vocation and was much loved within it, serving as a "den mother" and mentor to hundreds of young women who attended an Ursuline academy.

Cancer struck her brutally, and she spent the last months of her life bedridden. At that time, doctors, nurses, her sisters in community, and others took turns taking care of her.

Like Jesus, when Helen was helpless and no longer in charge, she was able to give life and meaning to others in a deeper way than she could when she was active and doing so many things for others.

There's a great lesson in this, not the least of which is how we view the terminally ill, the severely disabled, and the sick. There's also a lesson on how we might understand ourselves when we are ill, helpless, and in need of care from others.

The cross teaches us that we, like Jesus, give as much to others in our passivity as in our activity. When we are no longer in charge, beaten down by whatever, humiliated, suffering, and unable even to make ourselves understood by our loved ones, we are undergoing our passion and, like Jesus in his passion, have in that the opportunity to give our love and ourselves to others in a very deep way.

HOLY THURSDAY

This day will be a day of remembrance for you, which your future generations will celebrate with pilgrimage to the LORD; you will celebrate it as a statute forever.

EXODUS 12:14

In the Last Supper scene described in John's Gospel, the beloved disciple reclines with his head against Jesus' breast, able to hear his heartbeat. The beloved disciple, then, is the one who is attuned to the heartbeat of God and is looking out at the world from that vantage point.

In Luke's Gospel, Jesus admits that sometimes darkness seems to overpower grace and God seems powerless. Sometimes darkness just has its hour! Jesus' death was one of those hours, and the beloved disciple, like our Lord's mother, could do nothing but stand helpless inside and beneath that darkness and injustice. There was nothing to be done but to stand inside the helplessness.

By standing there, the beloved disciple also stands in solidarity with the millions of poor and victimized all over the world who can do nothing against their plight. When one stands in helplessness, when there's nothing possible to be done, one gives silent voice to human finitude, the deepest prayer possible at that moment.

Who is the beloved disciple? The beloved disciple is any person—woman, man, or child—who is intimate enough with Jesus to be attuned to the heartbeat of God and who then sees the world from that place of intimacy, prays from that place of intimacy, and sets off in love to seek the risen Lord and grasp the meaning of his empty tomb.

GOOD FRIDAY

For we do not have a high priest who is unable to sympathize with our
weaknesses, but one who has similarly been tested in every way, yet without sin.
HEBREWS 4:15

Nothing pushes us to the depths of heart and soul as does
humiliation. Just ask yourself these questions: What has given me
character? What has given me depth as a person? What has given me
deeper understanding? I suspect that the answer in every case will be
something you'd be ashamed to talk about, some stinging humiliation
whose pain and shame pushed you to a deeper place.

Drinking the cup of humiliation, accepting the cross is—according
to Jesus and according to what's most honest in our own experience—
what can bring us genuine glory, namely depth of heart, depth of soul,
and depth of understanding and compassion.

Like Jesus, we will all suffer humiliation in life, we will all drink
the cup, and it will make us deep. But then we have a critical choice.
Will this humiliation make us deep in compassion and understanding
or will it make us deep in anger and bitterness? That's the ultimate
moral choice we face in life—not just at the hour of death but countless
times. Good Friday, and what it asks of us, confronts us daily.

HOLY SATURDAY

"Do not be afraid! I know that you are seeking Jesus the crucified. He is not here, for he has been raised just as he said. Come and see the place where he lay."

MATTHEW 28:5–6

For Christians, Jesus' resurrection is the most monumental event, in our faith and otherwise, in history. To not understand the resurrection as the real physical transformation of a once-dead corpse is to rob it of some of its important meanings and perhaps of the deepest root of its credibility. There needs to be an empty tomb and a dead body returned to life. Why?

Not as some kind of miracle proof, but because of the Incarnation. To believe in the Incarnation is to believe that God was born into real physical flesh, lived in real physical flesh, died in real physical flesh, and rose in real physical flesh. To believe that the resurrection was only an event in the faith consciousness of the disciples—however real, rich, and radical that might be imagined—is to rob the Incarnation of its radical physical character and to fall into the kind of dualism that values spirit and denigrates the physical.

I believe that Jesus was literally raised from the dead. I also believe that this event was, as the rich insights within contemporary theology point out, highly spiritual: an event of faith, of changed consciousness, of new hope empowering a new charity and a new forgiveness. But it was also an event of changed atoms and of a changed dead body. It was radically physical, just as are all events that are part of the Incarnation, wherein God takes on real flesh.

EASTER
Gratitude

For you have died, and your life is hidden with Christ in God. When Christ your life appears, then you too will appear with him in glory.

COLOSSIANS 3:3–4

In John's Gospel, we are told the story of Lazarus and his sisters, Martha and Mary, who were very close friends of Jesus. Here's the story:

The sisters of Lazarus, Martha and Mary, sent word to Jesus that "the man you love is ill" with the implied request that Jesus should come heal Lazarus (John 11:3). Jesus' reaction is curious. He doesn't rush off to try to heal his close friend. Instead he remains where he is for two days longer while his friend dies. Then, after Lazarus has died, he sets off to visit him. As he approaches the village where Lazarus has died, he is met by Martha and then, later, by Mary. Each, in turn, asks him the question: "Why?" Why, since you loved this man, did you not come to save him from death?

Why is it that God invariably seems absent when bad things happen to good people? Why doesn't God rescue his loved ones and save them from pain and death? The answer to that question teaches a very important lesson, namely that God is not a God who ordinarily *rescues* us but is rather a God who *redeems* us. God doesn't ordinarily intervene to save us from humiliation, pain, and death. Rather, he redeems humiliation, pain, and death after the fact.

Simply put, Jesus treats Lazarus exactly the same way as God the Father treats Jesus. Our Savior is deeply and intimately loved by his Father, and yet his Father doesn't rescue him from humiliation, pain, and death. In Jesus' lowest hour—when he is humiliated, suffering, and dying on the cross—he's jeered by a thief being crucified who says, "Are you not the Messiah? Save yourself and us" (Luke 23:39). But there's no rescue. Instead, Jesus dies inside the humiliation and pain. God raises him only after he dies.

That is one of the key revelations inside of the resurrection, and it's the one we perhaps most misunderstand. We are forever predicating our faith on, and preaching, a rescuing God, a God who promises special exemptions to those of genuine faith. Have a genuine faith in Jesus and you will be spared from life's humiliations and pains! Have a genuine faith in Jesus and prosperity will come your way! Believe in the resurrection and rainbows will surround your life!

Jesus never promised us rescue, exemptions, immunity from cancer, or escape from death. Instead, he promised that, in the end, there will be redemption, vindication, immunity from suffering, and eternal life. In the meantime, we will experience the same kinds of humiliation, pain, and death that everyone else suffers.

The death and resurrection of Jesus reveal a redeeming God, not a rescuer.

God is not a God who ordinarily rescues us but is rather a God who redeems us.

MONDAY WITHIN THE OCTAVE OF EASTER

You have made known to me the paths of life; you will fill me with joy in your presence.

ACTS 2:28

The greatest miracles we ever experience have to do with gratuity, with love, with unfreezing a soul, with forgiveness. Our lives all end up incomplete, broken, and causing hurt to others because of our weaknesses, infidelities, sin, and malice. Ultimately, we know it can all wash clean again. There's redemption, new life after all the ways we've gone wrong in this world. And that redemption comes through forgiveness.

Forgiveness is the greatest miracle. Along with everlasting life, forgiveness is the real meaning of the resurrection of Jesus. There's nothing more godlike or miraculous than a moment of reconciliation, a moment of forgiveness.

It's for this reason that when the Gospels write about the resurrection of Jesus, their emphasis is on forgiveness. Luke's Gospel does not distinguish the announcement of the resurrection from the announcement of the forgiveness of sins. Forgiveness and resurrection are inextricably linked.

When you see warmth and love break through someone who has long been captive of a bitter and angry heart, you are seeing something that's not just another instance of normal life, of ordinary unfolding. You're seeing newness, redemption, resurrection, forgiveness.

And so, in the words of Benedictine monk Benoît Standaert: "Whenever we strive to bring a little more peace through justice here on earth and, in whatever form, change sadness into happiness, heal broken hearts, or assist the sick and the weak, we arrive directly at God, the God of the resurrection."

TUESDAY WITHIN THE OCTAVE OF EASTER

Jesus said to her, "Mary!" She turned and said to him in Hebrew, "Rabbouni," which means Teacher.

JOHN 20:16

In John's Gospel, the first words out of Jesus' mouth are an invitation that the entire Gospel then tries to answer: What are you looking for?

Jesus tells us we are looking for many things: living water that quenches our deepest thirst, a truth that sets us free, a rebirth to something above, a light that shines eternally. These images can seem abstract. What's the real kernel inside them?

Near the end of the Gospel we have that poignant, post-resurrection meeting between Jesus and Mary of Magdala. It takes place in a garden, a place where love takes place. Mary, carrying spices to embalm Jesus' dead body, goes searching for him on Easter morning. She meets him but doesn't recognize him. Supposing him to be the gardener, she asks him where she might find the body of the dead Jesus. Jesus replies by repeating the question with which he opened the Gospel: "Whom are you looking for?" Before she can answer, he gives the deepest answer to that question. He pronounces her name in love: "Mary!" In that very-particularized affirmation of love, he writes her name into heaven.

We are forever trying to give ourselves wholeness, but we cannot. We cannot self-justify. We cannot make ourselves immortal. We cannot write our own names into heaven. Only love casts out anxiety and, indeed, only a certain kind of love can give us substance.

Only God's love can write our names into heaven.

WEDNESDAY WITHIN THE OCTAVE OF EASTER

Peter said, "I have neither silver nor gold, but what I do have I give you: in the name of Jesus Christ the Nazorean, [rise and] walk."

ACTS 3:6

In the Gospels, Galilee is not simply a geographical location; it is first of all a place in the heart. Galilee refers to the dream and to the road of discipleship that the disciples once walked with Jesus and to that place and time when their hearts most burned with hope and enthusiasm. After the crucifixion, just when they feel that the dream is dead, that their faith is only fantasy, they are told to go back to the place where it all began: Galilee.

They do go back to Galilee, both to the geographical location and to that special place in their hearts where once burned the dream of discipleship. Just as promised, Jesus appears to them. He doesn't appear exactly as he was before, or as frequently as they would like him to, but he does appear as more than a ghost and a memory.

That is one of the essential messages of Easter: whenever we are discouraged in our faith, whenever our hopes seem to be crucified, we need to go back to Galilee, that is, back to the dream and the road of discipleship that we had embarked upon before things went wrong.

In one guise or another, Christ always meets us on the road to those places, burns holes in our hearts, explains our latest crucifixion to us, and once there, it all makes sense again.

THURSDAY WITHIN THE OCTAVE OF EASTER

[Peter quotes Moses as saying] "you are the children of the prophets and of the covenant that God made with your ancestors when he said to Abraham, 'In your offspring all the families of the earth shall be blessed.'"

ACTS 3:25

Everything that's good eventually gets scapegoated and crucified. How? By that curious, perverse dictate somehow innate within human life that assures that there's always someone or something that cannot leave well enough alone but, for reasons of its own, must hunt down and lash out at what's good.

What's good, what's of God, will always at some point be misunderstood, envied, hated, pursued, falsely accused, and eventually nailed to some cross. Everybody of Christ inevitably suffers the same fate as Jesus: death through misunderstanding, ignorance, and jealousy.

But there's a flip side as well: resurrection always eventually trumps crucifixion. What's good eventually triumphs. Thus, while nothing that's of God will avoid crucifixion, no body of Christ stays in the tomb for long. God always rolls back the stone and, soon enough, new life bursts forth and we see why that original life had to be crucified. Jesus said, "Was it not necessary that the Messiah should suffer these things and enter into his glory?" (Luke 24:26).

Resurrection invariably follows crucifixion. Every crucified body will rise again. Our hope takes its root in that.

FRIDAY WITHIN THE OCTAVE OF EASTER

There is no salvation through anyone else, nor is there any other name under
heaven given to the human race by which we are to be saved.

ACTS 4:12

In the resurrection we are assured that there are no doors
that are eternally closed. Every time we close a door, or one is closed
on us, God opens another for us. The resurrection assures us that
God never gives up on us, even if we give up on ourselves, that God
writes straight with the crooked lines of our lives, that we can forever
revirginize, regain lost innocence, become postsophisticated, and move
beyond bitterness.

In a scheme of things where Jesus breathes out forgiveness on those
who betray him and God raises dead bodies, we can begin to believe
that in the end all will be well, every manner of being will be well, and
everything—including our own lives—will eventually end sunny side
up.

However, the challenge of living this out is not just that of believing
that Jesus rose physically from the grave, but also, and perhaps even
more importantly, to believe that—no matter our age, mistakes,
betrayals, wounds, and deaths—we can begin each day afresh, virgin,
innocent again, a child, a moral infant, stunned at the newness of it all.

No matter what we've done, our future is forever pregnant with
wonderful new possibility. Resurrection is not just a question of one
day, after death, rising from the dead, but it is also about daily rising
from the many minigraves within which we so often find ourselves.

SATURDAY WITHIN THE OCTAVE OF EASTER

[Jesus] said to them, "Go into the whole world and proclaim the gospel to every creature."

MARK 16:15

We are saved by the death of Jesus! All Christians believe this. This is a central tenet within the Christian faith and the center of almost all Christian iconography. Jesus' death on a cross changed history forever.

But how does this work? How can one person's death ricochet through history, going backward and forward in time, being somehow beyond time, so as to affect past, present, and future all at the same time, as if that death was forever happening at the present moment? Is this simply some mystery and metaphysics inside of the Godhead that isn't meant to be understood within any of our normal categories?

Too often, I believe, the answer we were given was simply this: It's a mystery. Believe it. You don't have to understand it.

And there's wisdom in that. How we are washed clean in the blood of Christ is something we understand more in the gut than in the head. We know its truth, even when we don't understand it. Indeed, we know its truth so deeply that we risk our whole lives on it.

I wouldn't be a minister of the gospel and a priest today if I didn't believe that we are saved through the death of Jesus.

SECOND SUNDAY OF EASTER

For you have died, and your life is hidden with Christ in God. When Christ your life appears, then you too will appear with him in glory.

COLOSSIANS 3:4–5

Why doesn't God make things easier? Perhaps the most vexing faith question of all time is the problem of God's silence and his seeming indifference. Why does God allow evil? Why do bad things happen to good people?

The presence of evil in the world poses a deeper question. Why does God seem to be hidden? If God is so massively real, why do so many people not recognize, acknowledge, or care about his existence? Why do believers have to live, almost always it seems, on the edges of doubt? Why doesn't God make his existence clear, a fact beyond doubt? Why doesn't God silence his critics?

Evil exists because God respects freedom, both in nature and in human beings. When we are confronted with the problem of evil in the world, the conclusion we might draw is not that God doesn't exist or doesn't care, but rather that God respects and values freedom in a way that we don't.

God doesn't make things easier because God can't make things easier, at least not without making us and the world into something far less than we are. When God made us he gave us as much freedom, creativity, and spunk as was possible. He didn't play it safe but gave us as much godliness as he could without making us into gods ourselves. Simply put, in making us, God went so far as to give us a freedom that even he won't tamper with. That's risky, but as a parent, it seems God would rather risk than control, allow creativity outside of his influence than limit ingenuity, and tolerate the misuse of freedom than relate to robots. God is perceived as silent because he allows human freedom and ingenuity to be precisely what they are meant to be: noncoerced, even by God. God is not a frightened parent who needs to control, nor a threatened creator who kept what was best back for himself. God allows